Reviews

Intention is everything! Scripture teaches us over and over to set our minds, renew our minds, and choose joy. *Hope in the Waiting* is a 40-day resource to help you set your intention each day by providing you with a scripture, a word of encouragement, and a prayer. You won't be the same.

~Pastor Robb Schmidgall, Online Pastor, National Community Church

Hope in the Waiting is a faith-builder! It's a treasure trove of wisdom, encouragement, hope, and eye-opening truths. We loved it! They are stories about real life and how God meets us there. His heart is revealed on each page.

~ Pastor Dave & Alice Darroch, Senior Pastors, Spokane Dream Center

Lent is a season of hopeful anticipation, not only about what God has done for us, but what God can and will do in the future. *Hope in the Waiting* is a beautiful 40-day journey into the recognition that we not only are not alone in the waiting, but there is encouragement, strength, and power as we wait. It's a reminder that something is happening while we wait; God is at work as we anticipate His work!

~ Pastor Lyle Tard, Associate Pastor, National Community Church

Hope
In the Waiting

40 reflections and prayers
for the Lent season

Hope in the Waiting

40 reflections and prayers
for the Lent season

Edited by Barbara Hollace & Shalley Kim

Published by Hollace House Publishing Spokane Valley, Washington

Hope in the Waiting: 40 reflections and prayers for the Lent season

Copyright 2024 Barbara J. Hollace

All rights reserved.

No part of this publication may be reproduced, stored in a retrieval system, or transmitted in any form by any means, electronic, mechanical, photocopying, recording, or by any information retrieval or storage system without the express written permission of the author except in the case of excerpts used for critical review.

For more information about the book or authors, please email: barbara@barbarahollace.com.

All scripture quotations are the New International Version unless otherwise noted.

THE HOLY BIBLE, NEW INTERNATIONAL VERSION®, NIV® Copyright © 1973, 1978, 1984, 2011 by Biblica, Inc.® Used by permission. All rights reserved worldwide.; Scripture quotations marked NLT are taken from the *Holy Bible*, New Living Translation, copyright © 1996, 2004, 2015 by Tyndale House Foundation. Used by permission of Tyndale House Publishers, Inc., Carol Stream, Illinois 60188. All rights reserved.; Scripture taken from The Voice™. Copyright © 2008 by Ecclesia Bible Society. Used by permission. All rights reserved.; Scripture taken from the New King James Version®. Copyright © 1982 by Thomas Nelson. Used by permission. All rights reserved.

Book cover artwork: Anastassia Geiger

Book editing: Barbara Hollace, www.barbarahollace.com & Shalley Kim

Book layout/cover design: Ann Mathews

ISBN: 979-8-9854092-4-6

Printed in the United States of America

Dedication

Dedicated to National Community Church's Upper Zoom family – our spiritual brothers and sisters, and their families for generations yet to come.

All your children will be taught by the LORD,
and great will be their peace. Isaiah 54:13

In the Beginning…

There is a creation story to every great event and invention. The seed of an idea is dropped in your spirit by God and He watches it grow. God's dreams for us come true when we choose to press in and push through to victory.

2020 was a difficult year across the nation and around the world. With a runaway virus stalking us, there were great consequences. One of them meant staying at home unless you were an essential worker. Churches were closed, as were other large gatherings.

Just as in the days of Jesus and the formation of the early church, God would make a way for believers to gather. The power of prayer was not only evident but essential.

The seed planted and nurtured in a decade-long women's war room prayer group emerged as a virtual worldwide prayer gathering. Nicknamed "Upper Zoom" as we gathered together as believers on the Zoom platform, the maiden voyage took place on June 1, 2020, the day after Pentecost.

Hundreds of people gathered online to hear a short teaching and then pray together. The gatherings were igniting a passion to pray in the hearts of believers around the world. There was no stopping this prayer movement. God was taking ground back from the enemy.

During Lent 2022, a new direction was taken. The large Upper Zoom group continued to gather on Wednesdays, but smaller groups were formed. Starting with 15 members, our prayer pod continued to grow in attendance as friends shared with friends what the Holy Spirit was doing in our midst. Late in 2022, one of our members commented about the great wisdom in our group. Should this wisdom be shared in a book?

In the Spring of 2023, the Lord showed us His plan indeed was a book, a devotional. Each member could share a story of where there was a need and God met it. The book began to take shape. Since our prayer pod was born during the Lent season, it seemed appropriate this devotional would enter the world during Lent 2024, our second birthday.

May the 40 devotions you find on these pages spark a new flame in your soul. Jesus' walk to the cross was a path of suffering but so great was the "joy set before Him" that He endured the cross. Jesus saw you and me. Christ's compassion, love, forgiveness, mercy, and grace were on display on His path to Calvary. You are invited to encounter Jesus in a new way and find hope… in the waiting.

Foreword

A well-known phrase in the world of prayer movements has been circulating for years: "The person who has the most hope wields the greatest influence." National Community Church (NCC) Prayer has been dedicated to embodying this concept by striving to broker hope through numerous prayer expressions.

Building on this dedication, the authors of this devotional, who initially connected through a three-year online prayer movement called Upper Zoom, continue to carry forward this tradition. While this book is being released during Lent, its message is applicable to all seasons of life.

Hope in the Waiting is a concept that resonates deeply with the human experience and one that I have found as a prayer pastor affects every area of life. We often find ourselves waiting for so many things. We wait for salvation for loved ones. We wait for healing for ourselves and others. We wait for change. We wait for freedom. We wait for His kingdom to come to every aspect of our lives. We wait during seasons of grief, doubt, uncertainty, and despair. We wait to go from better to best. Everybody is waiting for something or someone.

We are even promised that those who "wait on the Lord will renew their strength."

What sets the Christian experience apart from many other forms of waiting is the profound belief that we don't simply wait in some ethereal void or empty universal space. Instead, we wait in the presence of our dear Lord, and in His presence, we find fullness of joy, hope, and purpose in the waiting.

In fact, Philippians tells us, "The Lord is near. Be anxious for nothing." Everyone loves to quote the "be anxious for nothing" part. But few people remember "the Lord is near." This should give us tremendous hope in the waiting because His presence is EVERYTHING.

Some may think solitary vigils are necessary for the best results during liturgical practices where "waiting" is commonplace, like Lent. However, in seasons of waiting, when we isolate ourselves to be with the Lord, His presence fills our entire being—body, soul, and spirit.

Our hope is grounded in His constant support and unwavering love. His presence and strength empower us to endure and stand firm, even during the longest waits.

The stories in this devotional will challenge, encourage, exhort, and console you. This book's personal, raw, and honest testimonies will make you feel seen, known, and heard.

The truth is that the victories in this book can become your victories, too.

We also dream that you will become part of the movement to broker hope, one prayer at a time.

Heidi Scanlon
Prayer Pastor Emeritus
National Community Church

But those who hope in the Lord will renew their strength. They will soar on wings like eagles; they will run and not grow weary, they will walk and not be faint. Isaiah 40:31

Day #1

THE WAITING

TODAY'S PASSAGE

See, I am doing a new thing! Now it springs up; do you not perceive it? I am making a way in the wilderness and streams in the wasteland. Isaiah 43:19

TODAY'S WORD

The Monstera Deliciosa Albo is a must-have for any serious plant collector. Knowing how much I desired to have one, a friend gave me an Albo that she propagated. I gave this beloved plant the prime spot in my house, a place with good sunlight and ventilation. Despite caring for it faithfully, it looked like it would remain a two-leaf plant forever. My confidence was shaken. Should I give up on the plant? No. Six months later, there were finally signs of growth. Sadly, my excitement turned to frustration as it took weeks for the new leaf to unfurl. To my relief, the plant finally unveiled a beautiful variegated leaf.

When it comes to my future, I have doubts and insecurities. Stuck in a long wilderness season, it has slowly eaten away at my confidence. Even though I don't see it, I try to be mindful that every day, pieces are falling into place. I don't have to be afraid that my prayers for a miracle are not being answered. Miracles don't necessarily come neatly packaged; they can be complicated – sometimes they're not evident to the human eye. In fact, for me, my miracle is that I haven't given up in the midst of suffering. I've been able to endure adversity because God has fought for me even when I couldn't fight for myself. The shaking in the wilderness caused my roots to grow thicker and deeper.

TODAY'S PRAYER

Father in heaven, help me to endure and run the race of life well. You see me and know me. I don't have to worry about tomorrow. I don't have to worry that I am missing out. Everything that I need, You will provide.

You are Jehovah Jireh. Bring peace to my mind and my heart so that I can seek first Your kingdom and Your righteousness (Matthew 6:33). Give me the strength to face hardship and adversity. You do not grow tired.

You give strength to the weary and increase the power of the weak. I put my hope in You. Renew my strength. Help me to run and not grow weary. Help me to walk and not faint (Isaiah 40:28-31).

I pray into my current situation. What little hope and faith I have, I plant in Your garden. I need You to be Lord over my circumstances. Resurrect the dead things. Tend the broken things. Do a new thing! May my life be fruitful.

I will remain in You as You remain in me. I know apart from You I can do nothing (John 15:5). Until my final breath, may I call upon You.

~ Shalley Kim

Day #2

DIRECTING OUR THOUGHTS

TODAY'S PASSAGE

Finally, brothers and sisters, whatever is true, whatever is noble, whatever is right, whatever is pure, whatever is lovely, whatever is admirable—if anything is excellent or praiseworthy—think about such things. Philippians 4:8

TODAY'S WORD

A Newsweek 2020 article stated that the average person thinks more than 6,000 thoughts a day, and according to the National Science Foundation, 80% of our thoughts are negative. Those thoughts generate quite a bit of mental traffic that needs to be managed and processed. Like an air traffic controller, we need to be careful which thoughts we allow to land in our minds and spirits because those thoughts are what we consume, meditate on, and ultimately become. Not every thought should be granted permission to land and may need to be redirected; especially the negative thoughts.

When my grandfather fell into a vat of 3,600° melted steel at work, I immediately prayed and thanked God for his healing, and also asked prayer warriors to pray. Because of his extensive burns, he wasn't expected to make it through the night. Each time a negative thought tried to enter my mind, I wouldn't let it land and instead thanked God for my grandfather's healing. Praise the Lord, he not only survived this horrific accident, but returned to work, ministered to other burn patients, and lived another 30 years.

The Word of God in Philippians 4:8 gives us a test to determine which thoughts should be permitted to land, which is whatever thoughts are true, noble, right, pure, lovely, or admirable, and anything that is excellent or praiseworthy. These are the things about which we should think and only allow them to land in our minds and spirits.

TODAY'S PRAYER

Dear Lord, we recognize that so much fear, anxiety, and stress result from thoughts we allow to enter our air space and rob us of our peace.

May we remember to use our God-given authority to control and direct our thoughts and renew our minds, focusing on things that are good, excellent, and praiseworthy.

May this redirection of our thoughts allow us to experience the rich peace of God that surpasses all understanding. In Jesus' name, amen.

~ Terrah A. Dews

Day #3

STEPPING INTO THE UNKNOWN

TODAY'S PASSAGE

By faith Abraham, when called to go to a place he would later receive as his inheritance, obeyed and went, even though he did not know where he was going. Hebrews 11:8

TODAY'S WORD

It was 2012, I was living the life I loved. I was raising my six-year-old, attending seminary, and blending my call to make art with my love of God. One day things all changed. My family lost our only source of income. Months went by with little hope. It was time for a Hail Mary prayer.

Dusting off my resume after seven years, my technical skills were stale. Believing my time in the business world was a thing of the past, God had a different plan. In faith I stepped into the unknown, asking God to bring me a job in three weeks, the start of a new semester. On the very last day, God brought me a professional job in the computer industry.

While journeying in this new world, God made room for both my art and a new "airport" ministry. As I traveled frequently, I was seated near people who were dying or dealing with a loved one's death who shared their story. God used me and my skills to further *His* kingdom, just not in the way I envisioned.

When we trust and lean into Him, God reminds us that *anything* is possible. He has a calling for our lives. We are invited to co-create with Him and listen carefully to His still, small voice. As God opens doors, we just have to listen and show up.

Is God inviting you to step into the unknown? Will you say "yes" to God?

TODAY'S PRAYER

Creator of all that is beautiful and good,

When all feels lost and we doubt our skills and gifts, when our compass is lost and GPS is out of range, help us to put the old maps together to build a new map. Show us the new signposts, the new way of thinking that leads us on the journey of the blueprint You created for us. Make a way and give us hope. Help our ears hear Your still small voice and help our eyes see You in all we do. Help our senses come alive as we stand in nature smelling the fresh crisp air, and tasting the goodness of all the fruits You bring to bear.

Be our close companion on this journey redirecting our course, when course corrections are needed. Let us know when our journey is supposed to shift to something new. When it's time to let go of the things that no longer serve us. Help us to live the dreams You have for us using all the skills we are gifted with for the glory of Your kingdom. Amen.

~ Jenna Marie Higgins

Day #4

USING YOUR VOICE FOR GOOD AND FOR GOD

TODAY'S PASSAGE

The tongue has the power of life and death, and those who love it will eat its fruit.
Proverbs 18:21

TODAY'S WORD

She was a tempestuous force, symphony of sound, and the heart of our neighborhood. Her voice, like a compass, would guide you to her location. In her 40s, she embarked on voice lessons. Her deep contralto resonated through walls, a testament to her vibrant spirit.

Her voice was a kaleidoscope of emotions. Joy danced in its notes, strength fortified its timbre, and energy pulsed through its very core. Crossed, it erupted like a tempest. Yet, she possessed a gift – the power to forgive, mend, and rebuild bridges shattered by anger. Not everyone could decipher this unique melody – she was either loved or hated.

As her only daughter, I stood in stark contrast, longing to be seen and heard. Molded and muted by her bustling workdays and relentless community service, I witnessed her boldness while being stifled in silence.

Though I shared boldly in my youth, as a newlywed, my husband urged restraint, annoyed at my speaking in church. My life was marked by constant ascent and descent, giving and retracting.

This inner turmoil led to pleasing others over trusting God. Leaving my 25-year marriage, I was depleted and worn. Through counseling and inner work, I learned to accept God's unwavering love and how to live out His call on my life.

God healed my childhood wounds and adulthood scars. Then God unlocked my voice and honed it for His purpose. Our fulfillment comes in discovering our identity in Him, as His voice expands through us. There's nothing like it!

TODAY'S PRAYER

Lord, take Your words and make them mine. Allow Your voice to speak through my mouth. May my lips proclaim Your goodness, and my actions declare Your mercy all the days left of my life.

Let me hear Your voice behind me, saying, "This is the way, walk in it" (Isaiah 30:21). Thank you that You have promised that You have begun a good work in me and You will finish it. May I be a voice of hope to others today. May I delight You every day.

"Let the words of my mouth and the meditation of my heart be acceptable in your sight, O Lord, my rock and my redeemer" (Psalm 19:14).

~Emra Smith

Day #5

WHERE DOES MY HELP COME FROM?

TODAY'S PASSAGE

I lift up my eyes to the mountains – where does my help come from? Psalm 121:1

TODAY'S WORD

Where do you turn for help? Psalm 121:2 reminds me, "My help comes from the Lord, the Maker of heaven and earth." God often sends volunteers – those who offer their services without cost or reward.

They are heaven-sent blessings, often in disguise. Volunteers may be passionate about a cause or just curious. Others want to step out of their comfort zone, or try something different.

When the need was greater than my resources, God sent volunteers to help me. Once I was in desperate need of help setting up and breaking down tents at a farmers' market. Another time teaching others how to prepare and preserve fresh produce. Sorting and packing duffle bags for children in foster care was an act of love and kindness. In turn, I have been a blessing to others, when I volunteered in a garden, or with children at church or summer camp. Even distributing water to marathon runners.

In nature, volunteer flowers, vegetables, herbs, vines, trees, and weeds spring up across the landscape. Windblown seeds take root. Bees pollinate flowers. Even squirrels and birds carry their treasures to new destinations.

My God will supply all your needs (Philippians 4:19). Unconditionally, God takes care of His people and His creation. Whether it's the summer heat or winter snow, He knows what we need. What a wonderful gift it is to witness the blessings of God. His sacrifice, love, compassion, and patience are without measure. His love is unconditional. God will meet your every need.

TODAY'S PRAYER

Heavenly Father, thank you for Your loving and tender way of teaching me how to recognize and appreciate the gift of volunteering through Your magnificent creation. Thank you for being my provider and helper when I was overwhelmed at work.

Faithfully, You sent the right person at the right time to fill a need even when I could not offer any financial appreciation. Thank you for sending Your Holy Spirit to remove the imagined barriers in my mind as You provided Your Word as a lamp for my feet and light to my path (Psalm 119:105).

Thank you for the challenges from busy volunteer rabbits, birds, and squirrels who both freely nibbled and eagerly contributed to my garden. They taught me how to pray in the midst of frustration rather than give up on gardening.

Thank you for reminding me to look to the mountains of Your grace rather than focus on the great valleys and distractions of life. Thank you for the wonderful pollinators who help the flowers bloom and the people who have volunteered their time and talent to teach me how to be a better hearer and doer of Your Word.

Thank you, Lord, for Your forgiving heart, Your faithfulness, and Your love which endures forever. Amen.

~ Liz Etim

Day #6

MY PROVIDER

TODAY'S PASSAGE

And my God will meet all your needs according to the riches of his glory in Christ Jesus.
Philippians 4:19

TODAY'S WORD

Koi (which means affection or love) fish are a delight to view. In Japanese culture, they symbolize strength, courage, and patience. Recently, I had the pleasure of spending time in a backyard garden with one of the most beautiful Koi ponds I have ever seen. I had the opportunity to feed them during my stay, and learned how attentive they are. When they see you, they rush over with mouths ajar, awaiting their food to be tossed into the water so they can eat.

What a life!

They swim around all day in a beautiful pond, resting, and awaiting their next meal. Kind of similar to our lives. We live our daily lives, sometimes we rest, and we are certainly dependent upon our God to provide our daily nourishment (Matthew 6:1), just as He said He would.

Like Koi depend on someone to feed them, we too must depend on God, our Provider. Life is certain to have ups and downs. What I know for sure is that God has never left me because He is my Provider. My needs have been met, time and time again.

And you know what, in times of my greatest uncertainty, God put me in places to serve others. Isn't that just like God to position us to serve (provide for) another while we wait?

Why? Because in our weakness, He is made strong (2 Corinthians 12:9) and He never fails to provide for His children.

TODAY'S PRAYER

God, thank you for being my Great Provider. When I don't know what to do or how to do it, just like the Koi, You strengthen me and infuse me with courage.

You love me and Your affection toward me is like no other. You have kept me, and I thank you that Your mercy and grace continue to chase me down and overtake any emotion that is not of You.

"Oh, to be kept by Jesus" is a prayer uttered by many saints. I thank you for keeping me when I did not know which way to turn. Thank you that You provide for my every need, every day.

Your Word says You have a good plan for my life (Jeremiah 29:11). Father, thank you that in times of uncertainty I will remain confident You are my Great Provider. I am protected by Your grace and mercy all the days of my life.

Thank you, Jesus. Your praise will continually stay in my mouth. Amen.

~Carolann Jones

Day #7

REMEMBER A BLESSING!

TODAY'S PASSAGE

David was greatly distressed because the men were talking of stoning him; each one was bitter in spirit because of his sons and daughters. But David found strength in the Lord his God. 1 Samuel 30:6b

TODAY'S WORD

Last year, I went through a prolonged season of isolation and loneliness at work. I'd just made a principled but unpopular decision that cost me the favor and companionship of my peers. I was first surprised and confused, then sorrowful by their response. The backlash became overwhelming, and it buffeted my fragile confidence. What could I do? I was alone.

David could relate. His closest companions threatened to kill him after returning home from battle and discovering that enemies had torched their homes and kidnapped their families. But David didn't ask his anguished and angry friends to spare him. Instead, a devastated David encouraged himself in the Lord. Then he sought God about the situation. David obeyed the Lord, and recovered all that was lost (1 Samuel 30:1-18 NLT).

Scripture doesn't tell us how David encouraged himself. But I bet he worshipped. It's who he was. When David shifted his focus from his pain to God's past faithfulness and power, faith told him that this time would be no different. That perfectly positioned him to pray, hear from God, and get the victory for everyone.

Imitating David taught me worship is still in every believer's DNA. And it is our strategy for overcoming in tough times. First, we remember a blessing, then praise, and finally, worship God for it. Repeat. Soon, we'll be in a better place to seek God, listen to Him, and learn how He will handle our situation.

TODAY'S PRAYER

Father, thank you for being with me in tough times. When it's hard to see or hear You, please help me to recall Your goodness and blessings toward me. When I do, I'll feel my faith rise to seek You and trust You for my victory.

If it doesn't come right away, then I still thank you for teaching me that worship is my weapon against self-pity because it shows me that I'm not alone. And it enables me to believe that You're moving on my behalf.

This means that my deliverance is at hand, and I praise you for it. In Jesus' name, I pray. Amen.

~ Nicole Thompson

Day #8

HEALING MIND AND BODY

TODAY'S PASSAGE

We have this hope as an anchor for the soul, firm and secure. It enters the inner sanctuary behind the curtain, where our forerunner, Jesus, has entered on our behalf.
Hebrews 6:19

TODAY'S WORD

The Lord has blessed me with relatively good health. But when I faced a significant surgery, fear greatly overwhelmed me. The physical and mental challenges of this journey surprised me.

When I didn't feel strong at all, I grew weary of people telling me to be strong. The five-hour surgery and all the potential risks and side effects, including the possibility of being disabled, stirred up fear in me. Fear became my companion. My medical team spoke of the certainty of excruciating pain. I didn't sign up for this! Most of all, I was afraid of overwhelming my husband with my constant care because recovery would take at least two years.

A few days before my surgery, while praying with a friend, Hebrews 6:19 jumped off the page. God was reminding me that His promises came with a guarantee. Taking hold of this hope in Jesus, the anchor of my soul, I was encouraged because He had already gone into the inner sanctuary on my behalf. Even though in my flesh it felt like I was going to death's door, I didn't need to be afraid. He would be waiting for me because Jesus is my High Priest forever.

The surgery was successful! From a wheelchair to a walker, then learning how to walk again. One year later, I put on hiking shoes to walk up rocky paths in the Holy Land! This is truly a testimony to God's faithfulness and His healing power in my body.

TODAY'S PRAYER

Jesus, my heart is full of gratitude and hope. Thank you for my family and friends who surrounded me with prayer and reminded me of Your promises. Fear tried to crush me. But I know I don't have to be afraid because I am never alone. Deuteronomy 31:6 reminds me that You will never leave me or forsake me.

I didn't face this surgery alone because You were with me. Even when I was under general anesthesia for hours, You took care of my bodily functions. You guided the surgeon's hands. Jesus, You comforted my loved ones. You are the Great Physician and my High Priest forever. Praise Your Holy Name!

Now I know I can climb mountains, physically and spiritually. I declare that I'm more than a conqueror in Jesus' name (Romans 8:37). You showed me that no weapon formed against me would prosper (Isaiah 54:17).

God, that is Your truth and it is where I stand. And I will walk out the rest of my life – from now until eternity in Your presence with the fullness of Your joy.

~ Linda Cawthon Griffin

Day #9

LOVE NEVER FAILS
(a simple truth to parents of adult children)

TODAY'S PASSAGE

And hope does not put us to shame, because God's love has been poured out into our hearts through the Holy Spirit, who has been given to us. Romans 5:5

TODAY'S WORD

A mother's soft "words of wisdom" and butterfly kisses do not solve every problem. When my son faced serious marital problems, Mom's remedies were ineffective for his adult owie. Our entire family was impacted, including my relationship with my daughter. Simple conversations became landmines of emotional strongholds.

Old divorce wounds, thought long gone, resurfaced as I felt responsible for the indelible blueprint it left on my young children. Explaining what they couldn't comprehend, only worsened things. Health, family traditions, peace, identity, and hope became challenges. The enemy's accusations are often in the areas of fear, shame, and blame. My family was immobilized because we couldn't hear each other's heart stories. Still, I wanted their understanding. But love keeps no record of being wronged or hurt (1 Corinthians 13).

Satan may score, but he can't win! God's love defeated him through the cross (Isaiah 53:4-6). The prodigal son returned, welcomed by his [brokenhearted] father who simply loved him (Luke 15:17-22). The father didn't seek his own rights or needs.

After months, I came to my spiritual senses. My emotions had blinded me from seeing my daughter's hurt, which was compounded by thinking she should see mine. *Ouch!* I acknowledged her pain. Letting go of *my* rights was healing. God's way *is* love and is always higher than ours. Wallowing in self-pity or self-defense halts our healing. Love is the cure for Mom guilt.

When I stopped believing the lies that I was the responsible martyr, the blame game ceased.

TODAY'S PRAYER

Father, thank you for the gift of children and grandchildren. Please help us to listen better as parents and surrender our own hurts and shortcomings to You. Let us not lean on our own understanding (Proverbs 3:5-6).

Thank you that when we miss the mark, You restore us wholly, without blame, guilt, or shame. Holy Spirit, we yield to You when things feel impossible when parenting adult children, because nothing is impossible with You. Let us be reminded that love never ever fails (1 Corinthians 13:8).

And like You, Lord, we have the capacity to love and forgive unconditionally, without keeping score. Lastly, help us as parents to forgive ourselves, as we continue to grow in Your love. Amen.

~Greta McHaney-Trice

Day #10
CHANGING EXPECTATIONS

TODAY'S PASSAGE

Now to him who is able to do immeasurably more than all we ask or imagine, according to his power that is at work within us. Ephesians 3:20

TODAY'S WORD

Often we ask and expect God to intervene in troubling or critical times in our lives. Even during everyday activities, He is with us, ordering our steps and guiding us. Recently, I had an experience that highlighted this.

Going into a restaurant to get a bite to eat, I discovered all the tables were occupied. So, I took a seat at the bar next to an older gentleman. After exchanging pleasantries, he began to share that his wife was in the hospital dying of cancer, his son had just lost a finger in an industrial accident, and his daughter was in the middle of a messy divorce. When the man sought solace from his priest, he was told that God never gives you more than you can bear. It was clear this gentleman did not find comfort in those words.

I shared that my reading of the same scripture (1 Corinthians 10:13) was that whatever you face God will equip you to handle. Difficult times are prime opportunities to yield to the temptation of doubting God's faithfulness to give us what we need to navigate troubles successfully. He expressed his thanks for the comfort in those words. As the man left he said, "You are my angel." Although not what I expected, the simple everyday act of getting a meal became an opportunity for me to minister to someone in need.

TODAY'S PRAYER

Gracious Lord, thank you for ordering my steps each day. Help me to remember that just as You said, "I am with you," to Isaac (Genesis 26:24), Jacob (Genesis 28:15), Moses (Exodus 3:12), the children of Israel (Isaiah 43:5), and Jeremiah (Jeremiah 1:8), You are with me providing all that I need.

Help me to expect and recognize Your hand in the mundane activities of my day, knowing that Your guidance and protection are present in the seen and unseen. All these blessings we ask in the name of Your son, Jesus. Amen.

~ Sharon McWilliams

Day #11

THE RESOLVE IN THE MIDDLE OF REJECTION

TODAY'S PASSAGE

Two are better than one, because they have a good return for their labor. Ecclesiastes 4:9

TODAY'S WORD

Should I sleep through prayer this morning? It was a difficult decision.

Like a stubborn toddler entrenched in her terrible twos, I could have chosen not to go. However, it was the last gathering of the year for the group I'd helped start only months earlier, and that seemed distasteful.

I was mad. Angry. Enraged. The night before I had received another rejection letter. It was the straw that broke the camel's back, but unlike past rejections, there was no place to run. I'd fallen in love with the practice of writing from the day my mother first put a pencil in my hand, but it had failed me. So, I went to prayer.

One of the women who was leading the group that day spoke of the deep disappointment she'd felt while trying to do the one thing God had told her. As good as I've known God to be, I was still surprised He would put that on her heart to share.

When the line opened up for prayer, I had no choice but to pray about the pain I was in. God met me there.

I also felt a new resolve develop as I asked God what He wanted to do with this last rejection. Nine months after my prayer pod prayed for me, I published *Selah: A Study of 1 and 2 Samuel*. I am so thankful He sent me these Spirit-filled sisters.

TODAY'S PRAYER

Jesus, today we pray that You would fill us with a renewed resolve to move in obedience despite the rejection and resistance that attempt to build in our hearts.

We trust that regardless of what warfare awaits as we travel this road, we will see it through. There will be many ways we will find our dependence upon Your strength, and rejoice in the great revelation You give us in the midst of it. It will be worth it!

We pray for a godly community, particularly for the one who reads this.

Your Word says,

"Two are better than one, because they have a good return for their labor: If either of them falls down, one can help the other up. But pity anyone who falls and has no one to help them up" (Ecclesiastes 4:9-10).

We thank you for the words of comfort and conviction You send through our friends and family. Help us learn how to recognize when it is Your voice, how to pray through the pain, and how to move forward. In Your holy name, we pray, amen.

~Liv Dooley

Day #12

SURRENDERING ME

TODAY'S WORD

He must increase and I must decrease. John 3:30

TODAY'S WORD

John the Baptist's words spoken after Jesus' baptism are a reminder to *each* of us that everything – our work, ministry, and relationships are not about us, but about Jesus. The summer of 2023, I learned this lesson quite vividly while visiting Zambia and discovering Abba's power in a whole new way. The Holy Spirit was preparing the terrain before my arrival.

After a two-hour drive from the airport, I met Bishop and "the family" with exuberant joy, worship, and dancing from children and adults alike. Their joy was contagious and filled me up the first night along with a magnificent African sunset only God can paint. The next day included learning the names of the children (47 total), reading them a story from *The Circle Maker for Children*, and answering their questions about scripture. Then we had lunch together.

Afterwards, they taught me a song in Bemba (their native language) even though the older ones spoke English. It was such a simple day. Everything I had learned, studied, taught, and lived about my Savior was being used in this place. When the next opportunity came, there was no preparation time. None was needed because Abba had been preparing me my whole life for this moment.

As each day progressed, Jesus was increasing and I was decreasing, just as the apostle John wrote. Abba was teaching me that lessons learned in one season can reappear in another season to bring new truth to walk in.

TODAY'S PRAYER

Abba, I ask that as each person examines themselves during this Lenten season, we would listen to You and read Your Word.

May we hold its truth in our hearts, letting it soak into our souls as it changes our temptation to do what we want. Help us, Lord Jesus, to lean upon You and Your truth.

Give us grace each day as we walk this journey with You. Holy Spirit, give us strength that is not our own and wisdom to speak love and light in the darkness where we live and work.

I love you, Adonai, my friend and companion. May You increase a hundredfold in each of us this day.

~JoEllen Delamatta

Day #13
WALKING IN THE WORD

TODAY'S PASSAGE

Blessed is the one who does not walk in step with the wicked or stand in the way that sinners take or sit in the company of mockers. Psalm 1:1

TODAY'S WORD

God favors and prospers us if we passionately and habitually meditate on His Word.

Recently, my husband and I moved our daughter to college, our last child to leave home. It's been bittersweet. For 22+ years, we raised our two kids. Suddenly, our home and lives became quieter. I missed her voice, presence, and the joy she exuded. Feeling sad I pondered, "Did I do enough to prepare her for life?"

As a mother, my kids are my greatest accomplishment. I was proud to disciple them in their relationship with the Lord. Yet they still have unique struggles. Afraid of exposing them to hardship, I was overprotective, thinking I was doing the right thing. Self-correcting for the trauma I experienced as a child. God revealed being motivated by fear is really unbelief. Separation from my daughter drove me to meditate on the Word.

That's when I saw this root of unbelief. I distrusted God's ability to care for my children. It was a sobering realization. My heart sank with regret. God reminded me of Psalm 1 and its promise of blessing as I dug deep in His Word. I resisted partnering with unbelief. His Word protected my heart from walking in step with wickedness.

TODAY'S PRAYER

Lord, I come today with many things in my heart. But I recognize that You are Lord. You are worthy of all I am and all I have. I lay it all at Your feet. I praise and worship you today. I admit I haven't always obeyed Your Word.

By hiding Your Word in my heart, I am protected from sinning against You (Psalm 119:11). Sometimes I self-righteously think I have the answers and judge others for being wicked, but I miss the wickedness in my own heart.

My heart is deceitful (Jeremiah 17:9, Romans 7:9). The truth is sometimes I think I'm doing the right thing but it's not what You want.

Drive me to seek You more and meditate on Your Word so You can examine my heart for places I can't see where I am harboring wickedness (Psalm 139:23-24). Your Word promises that when I confess (say I'm wrong) and repent (decide not to do that wrong anymore), You will forgive me and not hold it against me (1 John 1:9).

I confess _____ and ask You to clean my heart and give me a fresh start so I can walk in righteousness. I believe You have done it. In Jesus' name, amen.

~Morenike Ogebe

Day #14

A SEASON OF RESTORATION

TODAY'S PASSAGE

A shoot will come up from the stump of Jesse; from his roots a Branch will bear fruit.
Isaiah 11:1

TODAY'S WORD

"If you haven't had a storm in your life, wait a while." As a child, I did not quite understand the significance of my mother's statement. As a "seasoned" adult, I am keenly aware of its substance.

Seven years ago, I experienced a crisis that reshaped my faith. We lost our only son, David, to violence on January 1, 2017. I thought my own life had ended. I was angry and did not understand why my son, who was so peaceful, had his life end this way.

God was my foundation. I couldn't walk away from Him. My life was devoted to helping others. However, I proclaimed I would stay home, pray, and read His Word but avoid His people. I would not talk to anyone about God or try to justify how a loving God allowed such a horrible thing to happen.

Israel knew the sting of enslavement in Egypt and the pangs of exile in Babylon. Isaiah reminded them there was a promise even in their moments of complete despair. I was also encouraged by these words. God restored my hope by reminding me David knew Him. However, there were others at 27 years old that did not. God was calling me to introduce them to the "shoot" that would come up from the stump of Jesse, Jesus!

In this season of Lent, the Lord is reminding us there is a promise. His name is Jesus.

TODAY'S PRAYER

Lord, restore our hope in the fulfillment of Your promise in our lives. Remind us through John 1:5 that You are the light that shines in the darkness, and the darkness cannot overcome You.

Help us to move toward You; despite how bad things may seem or how bad things get, there is always hope. God does not leave us hopeless.

We anxiously await the day when nature is transformed, and the original intention of our Creator will be evident. This plan will establish the most vulnerable of our world, a child, to lead the most feared of creatures (Isaiah 11:6).

We wait for the return of Jesus, when the world will be righted, as You intended, dear Lord. That is our hope. Our hope is Jesus!

Lord, help our holy imagination to be ignited amid the current chaos. May we see as You see and participate in Your plan. In Jesus' name, amen.

~Pastor Valarie Grimes

Day #15

BE STILL

TODAY'S PASSAGE

The Lord will fight for you; you need only be still. Exodus 14:14

TODAY'S WORD

As an obstetrician and gynecologist, I know pregnancies, deliveries, and surgeries do not always go as planned. Everything has an innate risk. While most of the time things go well, sometimes complications arise.

When I wake up at about 4 a.m., I am thinking about my patients, my surgery schedule, and the babies I have delivered. I always want my patients and/or their babies to be healthy. My prayer often is that "I do no harm" and not miss something. During both difficult and exciting moments in their lives, I want to be an educator, confidant, and source of encouragement to my patients and colleagues.

Thinking about the past and what I could have done differently or worrying about the week ahead, I remind myself that God is in control. He cares for me and my patients. Although I am a competent, well-trained, experienced physician, it is God who is all-powerful.

God is the one who supports, inspires, comforts, and sustains us. When we have given our all, in support of the goals He has placed on our hearts, He gives us rest. God is in control of our lives. If we are lost, exhausted, or overwhelmed, we must pray. When we pray, meditate, or sleep (all ways of being still in God's presence), God will send peace, comfort, and eventually, deliverance.

God has us and we need not worry. He is fighting for you and me.

TODAY'S PRAYER

The Lord is my shepherd, I lack nothing.

He makes me lie down in green pastures,

He leads me beside quiet waters,

He refreshes my soul.

He guides me along the right paths for his name's sake (Psalm 23:1-3).

Dear Lord,

Please help us to remain open to Your constant encouragement and direction in our lives. Help us to know what is ours to do. Once we have done all we can to accomplish the work You have placed in our hearts, please give us rest and Your peace.

In Jesus' name we pray, amen.

~ Kieu Smith

Day #16

LOST AND FOUND

TODAY'S PASSAGE

But the Pharisees and the teachers of the law muttered, "This man welcomes sinners and eats with them." Luke 15:2

TODAY'S WORD

After being stored away for six years, I was preparing to move my mother's beautiful mahogany credenza. It would crown my living room and be a daily reminder of Mom. But there was a problem. The credenza had been locked for storing and the skeleton keys to open it were missing. I checked and re-checked every logical place I could have put them with no success.

"Lord," I prayed, "I don't know where those keys are but You do."

Minutes later, I rejoiced at God's provision — miraculously, He led me right to them. In that moment, my rejoicing was not solely for the joy of the keys. Much more than that, I rejoiced for the reassurance of God's promise to me.

I had been crying out to God over my lost son, when I heard a whisper, "Drew is not lost forever." Since then, God has been confirming these words again and again — as, by His grace, He has led me to find lost items of every kind.

In Luke 15, as Jesus mingled with tax collectors and sinners, He recounted stories of a good shepherd who joyfully locates a lost sheep, a widow's lost and found coin, and a father's rejoicing when his lost son is found. Truly, Jesus came to seek and save the lost.

Are you burdened by a lost loved one? S/he is not lost to Jesus. He is more than able to *guard what you have entrusted to Him until that day* (2 Timothy 1:12).

TODAY'S PASSAGE

Father God, thank you that You are our light and our salvation. We do not have to fear when we cannot see. You are the strength of our life and we don't have to be afraid of the unknown (Psalm 27:1).

I pray for lost children, parents, siblings, friends, and family members. Thank you that You are El Roi, the God who sees each one (Genesis 16:14-15) and they are not lost to You. Jesus, thank you that You came to seek and save the lost (Luke 19:10).

I pray for Your protection over our loved ones, that You preserve them (Psalm 91), strengthen them, and protect them from the evil one. Direct their hearts into Your love and Christ's perseverance. (2 Thessalonians 3:3,5).

Father, please fill them with the knowledge of Your will in all spiritual wisdom and understanding, that they may live lives worthy of You and please You in every way: bearing fruit in every good work and growing in their knowledge of You (Colossians 1:9-10).

Thank you that they are safe in Your arms. In Jesus' name, amen.

~ Adrienne Howell

Day #17

GOD KNOWS MY NAME

TODAY'S PASSAGE

But now, this is what the LORD says – he who created you, Jacob, he who formed you, Israel: "Do not fear, for I have redeemed you; I have summoned you by name; you are mine."
Isaiah 43:1

TODAY'S WORD

Your name is important. It's how people greet you and remember you. There is only one you. There are no duplicates, even if you have an identical twin. Most importantly, God wrote a book about your life before you were born and your name was written at the top of the page. Psalm 139:13 says, "For you created my inmost being; you knit me together in my mother's womb." The Lord says, "Do not fear." Why? Because God has redeemed us. He calls us by name and says we belong to Him. This is a great comfort to those who are lonely, weary, lost, and even those who are happy and filled with joy. I can count on Him to never leave me or forsake me (Deuteronomy 31:8). I will always belong somewhere, close to my Father's heart.

Growing up as a kid, I had a short name, long name, and nickname. Our name is part of our identity. In my lifetime, I have known what it's like to be single, married, and also a widow… twice. My last name has changed several times, but in my heavenly Father's eyes my name remains the same, His Beloved.

No matter what I face in the world, good times, hard times, mountains or valleys, my hope rests in the nail-scarred hands of Jesus, my Lord and Savior. The only debt I owe is a debt of love to God who created me.

TODAY'S PRAYER

Heavenly Father, thank you for the gift of Your great love. Your son, Jesus, is the greatest gift of all. Because of Jesus, I can face my problems today with the hope of a brighter tomorrow.

When I am feeling alone, You remind me that You know my name. I am not lost, even if I am directionally challenged, because my soul knows heaven is my home. When I have lost someone I loved, You remind me that Your love never fails (1 Corinthians 13:8).

My heart may be broken by my circumstances but my hope is secure in You. Jesus, You died that I might live. Heaven is my home and earth is a place where I am called to walk with You and live for Your honor and glory.

When I pass through the waters, You will be with me; and when I pass through the rivers, they will not sweep over me. When I walk through the fire, I will not be burned; the flames will not set me ablaze (Isaiah 43:2).

Lord, I know that You will lead me through every adversity. No matter how high the mountain or how deep the valley, Your grace, mercy, and peace will be my companions.

For those who are lost, who have lost sight of who they are, help them remember that You, heavenly Father, know their name and they are forever loved by You. Lead us by Your powerful, yet gentle hand, now, and for all eternity. Amen.

~ Barbara Hollace

Day #18

JOY IN THE MORNING

TODAY'S PASSAGE

I delight greatly in the Lord; my soul rejoices in my God. For he has clothed me with garments of salvation and arrayed me in a robe of his righteousness. Isaiah 61:10

TODAY'S WORD

I needed a break! Doctor's appointments were innumerable since I was diagnosed with incurable uterine cancer in 2021. Two years later, I needed surgery for cataracts.

The day of surgery, I arrived at the medical center, tired and feeling overwhelmed. In all my trials and testing, the Lord has always been there to comfort and encourage me, saying, "I am with you," so I needed to give God some praise! In my inner man, I began to call on His name and praise Him.

While my daughter and I were waiting, the doors swung open, and my name was called. Two young people introduced themselves as "Jericho and Majesty," and said, "We are your attending nurses."

"Wait a minute! Repeat your names! Are you for real? You're not making this up, are you?"

As they escorted me to prepare for surgery I said, "My Father, You are always with me. 'If the Eternal had not come to my rescue, my soul would have descended to the Land where death silences every voice' (Psalm 94:17 VOICE). You have shown up again! The Lord has sent Jericho and Majesty to take care of me!" Thank you, Jesus!

During the drive home, my daughter said, "Mom, did you know that Jesus healed a blind man on the road to Jericho?" (Luke 18:35-43). And I said, "Joy comes in the morning."

TODAY'S PRAYER

My prayer and praise to God is to thank Him. For You have taken note of my journey through life, caught each of my tears in Your bottle. I am bound by Your promise, O God. My life is my offering of thanksgiving to You. "For You have saved my soul from the darkness of death, steadied my feet from stumbling so I might continue to walk before God embraced in the light of the living" (Psalm 56:13 VOICE).

As a child I was taught the holy scriptures, to trust in the Lord with all my heart, to hold on to God's unchanging hand. When I was tempted to hold on to doubt and fear, my dad would remind me of the Word of God, "Lord, to whom shall we go? You have the words of eternal life" (John 6:68).

The Lord is our Rock, our great high tower.

Father, You are with me and will never leave me. Your word is a lamp unto my feet and light unto my path (Psalm 119:105). Lord, every day I wake up is a gift from You. Thank you for joy!

The Mighty God, the Eternal God of past, present, and future has blessed us, He has redeemed us and sealed us by His Spirit. To Him be all glory, honor, domination, power, and majesty forever and ever, amen.

~ G Washington

Day #19

BEAUTIFULLY IN OVER MY HEAD

TODAY'S PASSAGE

When you pass through the waters, I will be with you; and when you pass through the rivers, they will not sweep over you. When you walk through the fire, you will not be burned; the flames will not set you ablaze. Isaiah 43:2

TODAY'S WORD

I know what it's like to be broken. I've walked through abuse, addictions, loss, and homelessness.

While I was knocking on death's door, God was knocking on mine. Finally, after endless attempts to escape my life's mess, I opened the door and let God in. I found Jesus but my problems didn't go away. There were many stumbles on my journey. I battled with anger and fear. I was angry at God for allowing difficult times, and living in fear that it was always going to be this way.

I remembered I am not alone in my suffering. As we walk through this Lenten season, we are reminded that Jesus suffered on the cross. He is with us through our hardest circumstances. The more we seek Him through the storms, we realize His living water strengthens us and heals us from our past traumas. Every time the Lord brings victory in our lives, we are empowered to face the next test. With every challenge, you become stronger in faith and character. We go through hard times to prepare us to be able to bring others the love and hope we have in Christ. Without challenges, we would never grow.

When you find this place of trusting the Lord, you can be fully submerged in His presence and breathe freely even when you're under water. When you encounter your next storm, dive in the waters head first. When the storm passes, you'll see you were beautifully in over your head.

TODAY'S PRAYER

Lord, You are my God, I crave and thirst for You. Please help me turn to You alone when I cannot keep my head above water. My whole being longs for You, for Your living water.

Help me realize that I can surround myself in Your presence during life's storms. To totally submerge myself in faith and trust in You. Forgive me when I don't trust You fully.

When I'm operating in fear and flailing in the waves, Holy Spirit, wash over me and bring the peace that only You can give. Help strengthen me to keep my eyes on You and know that You are a good Father and will not forsake me.

I trust You when You lead me into deeper waters. You are preparing me for growth and greater things.

Give me a spirit of gratitude for the challenges and for what You are doing in them. Thank you for loving me through all the hard things.

~ Anastassia Geiger

Day #20

FEED MY SHEEP

TODAY'S PASSAGE

When they had finished eating, Jesus said to Simon Peter, "Simon son of John, do you love me more than these?" "Yes, Lord," he said, "you know that I love you." Jesus said, "Feed my lambs." John 21:15

TODAY'S WORD

Ever wonder why God refers to us as His sheep?

A shepherd's life calling is to tend to, protect, defend, guide, nurture, and lead his flock.

Sheep need a shepherd as they tend to go astray.

Although born a pastor's kid (PK), or rather a theologian's offspring (TO), I definitely fell into the "black sheep" category. I am so grateful I have a loving shepherd who for years, despite my wandering and reckless disobedience, protected me, as I got myself into *a lot* of messy situations. Just ask my family!

Sheep also know their shepherd's voice. I did not listen to His voice or *know* His voice most of my life, yet He never gave up on me. A very late bloomer, I learned everything the hard way; not looking to anyone for guidance, certainly not to the Bible. John 10:16 says, "I have other sheep that are not of this sheep pen. I must bring them also. They too will listen to my voice, and there shall be one flock and one shepherd."

He eventually led me to my God-given passion (people) & current vocation – Real Estate – where I now get to "feed His sheep" daily. Praise God He *never* gave up on me and now dwells in me.

TODAY'S PRAYER

Thank you, Lord, for never giving up on me. Jesus, speak to us. Open our ears to hear Your still, quiet voice. "The Lord is my Shepherd. I shall not want. He makes me lie down in green pastures. He leads me beside still waters. He restores my soul. Thy rod and thy staff comfort me" (Psalm 23:1-2, 4b).

Lord Jesus, like sheep, we need a shepherd. Thank you for being our good, good Shepherd. You know us and love us. Lead us to still waters so we can hear Your voice and follow You.

Guide us to abide in You. Make us sensitive to Your spirit. Create in us a passion to follow You.

May we step out in faith and serve You by loving our neighbors and feeding Your sheep. Amen.

~JoJo Stansfield

Day #21

GOD SHOWS UP IN THE DARKEST VALLEY

TODAY'S PASSAGE

Even though I walk through the darkest valley, I will fear no evil, for you are with me: your rod and your staff, they comfort me. Psalm 23:4

TODAY'S WORD

As a Nurse Executive, one of my jobs is to make sure the operations of the Emergency Department run smoothly. The nursing shortage has been around for a while, but the pandemic exacerbated it. Hospitals were recruiting nurses from each other with large monetary rewards. This made things even worse. We were faced with critical shortages in critical areas like the Emergency Department.

I've always been a praying person, but in this situation, I felt it necessary to call key leaders together to draw a circle around what looked impossible. I asked the Chief Nursing Officer and my fellow Nursing Directors if they would meet for early morning prayer once a week. They felt the same desperation I did, so they said yes!

We met every Friday in the hospital chapel, and within days, God showed up and our prayers were answered.

The Federal Emergency Management Agency (FEMA) deployed a large number of nurses to work at our hospital for 60 days. The Emergency Department had more than enough nurses to care for the patients during the peak of the covid surge in the fall of 2021. This is a testimony of how God walks with us through the darkest valley. We don't have to fear, God is with us. God shows up in dark valleys with answers to our most pressing prayers.

TODAY'S PRAYER

Dear God,

Thank you for not leaving me when I face impossible situations, when I want to give up, when I feel helpless, and when I don't have the answers. Your Word tells me all things are possible to the one who believes (Mark 9:23).

During difficult times, I sometimes feel like my faith is faltering. Lord, please give me the faith I need to face every difficulty. Lord, I do believe but help my unbelief (Mark 9:24).

When the enemy comes in like a flood, God, You will raise up a standard against my enemy (Isaiah 59:19). When I pass through deep waters, God, You will be with me.

When I go through the rivers of difficulty, I will not drown. When I walk through the fire of oppression, I will not be burned up. Nothing can separate me from the love of God (Isaiah 43:2).

Lord, we pray a special prayer for caregivers who sometimes feel like they need someone to care for them. Lord, thank you for comforting us all when we need it most in the darkest valley. Amen.

~ Penne Allison

Day #22
DAILY JOY

TODAY'S PASSAGE

Give thanks in all circumstances; for this is God's will for you in Christ Jesus.
1 Thessalonians 5:18

TODAY'S WORD

Where to go? What to do? Why am I here? How can I serve others? These are the questions of my life. There are ups and downs. Highs and lows. Hills and valleys.

Seek God first with all your heart, and joy follows. When we're filled with God's love, forgiveness, mercy, and grace, there's an indescribable joy. The recipe to true fulfillment is daily prayer, affirmation, and scripture.

1 Cup of Praying Continually: Before my feet hit the floor, prayer is on both my conscious and subconscious mind. Throughout the day, I sacredly pause to pray for others and self for the "big" and "small."

1 Cup of Giving Thanks: Uttering gratitude to start the day and throughout the day, about anything and everything. With thanksgiving, serving unconditionally.

1 Cup of the Word of God: God's Word helps us live out our purpose with the Holy Spirit's guidance. Memorizing scripture and placing verses where I can see them feeds my soul.

Overcoming odds and not beating to the drum of the world's metrics has been an on-going challenge for me. However, with the aforementioned recipe, I experience miracles daily.

On life's journey, I've realized success comes when I make God's desires, my desires. Finding fulfillment in family, clothes, physical/mental prowess, vacation, or new adventures doesn't compare to the love and daily joy found in Christ. God is my ultimate authority. He is Jehovah Jireh, my provider. Daily joy is found in Jesus. He is the greatest gift of all.

TODAY'S PRAYER

Rejoice always, pray continually, and give thanks through all circumstances (1 Thessalonians 5:16-18). This is God's will for our lives. Your desire is for us to be filled with joy and gratitude through the ebb and flow of life.

When times are difficult and challenging, You are good. When times are exciting and we're floating and glowing with awe and blessings, God, You are good. Every day is a miracle because You are the Miracle Worker.

We rejoice because You are the Joy Giver. We pray and You hear our cry for help. It's a testimony to Your faithfulness. I have a reason to rejoice and give thanks. May we bask in Your presence, God. May we surrender to Your will and not our own.

God, we are grateful for everything! Nature. A walk. Meeting with a dear friend. Getting a good laugh. Eating a healthy meal. Dancing. Listening to good music. Exercising. Seeking You with our whole heart. We praise you, Lord. In Jesus' name, amen.

~ Octavia Shaw-Williams

Day #23

BREATHE ON ME, HOLY SPIRIT

TODAY'S PASSAGE

And with that he breathed on them and said, "Receive the Holy Spirit." John 20:22

TODAY'S WORD

For over a year, our Monday night prayer warriors rallied in prayer for our friend, urging the heavens to open and grace her with a place on the lung transplant list (double lung transplant). Miraculously, the day arrived when she received the good news – she was finally on the list. The journey ahead was daunting, filled with uncertainties, yet her faith stood unshaken.

Her path post-surgery was far from smooth. Complications arose, testing her resolve and stretching her faith to its limits. The true essence of faith is not revealed in the absence of challenges, but in the unwavering courage to face them.

Through pain and tears she held onto her faith, trusting in the Lord's plan even when it seemed incomprehensible. She found strength in prayer, solace in the scriptures, and courage in the unwavering support of her Monday night prayer warriors.

The breath of life that sustained her was not just air filling her lungs but the very essence of God, reminding her that she was not alone in her battle.

There will be moments when we, too, need that divine breath. Our challenges may leave us breathless. As we hold on to our faith, we find the strength to face life's uncertainties, and the courage to persevere through the storms.

May our friend's story be a beacon of hope. Even in the face of complications, the power of the Holy Spirit can move mountains, heal, and breathe life into the darkest of moments.

TODAY'S PRAYER

Dear Lord, we thank you for our friend, a testament to Your enduring grace and the power of faith. In moments of difficulty and despair, may we lean on You, knowing that with each inhale, we receive the strength to persevere.

In John 20:21-22, as Jesus breathed upon His disciples, imparting the Holy Spirit, breathe on us anew today. May we live a renewed life filled with divine empowerment.

Help us, Lord, to face challenges with unwavering faith, trusting in Your plan even when it seems beyond our understanding.

Breathe on us, Lord, and fill our spirits with Your peace, Your strength, and Your everlasting love. In Jesus' name, we pray.

~Rosalind Able

Day #24

A TIME OF REFRESHING

TODAY'S PASSAGE

Repent, then, and turn to God, so that your sins may be wiped out, that times of refreshing may come from the Lord. Acts 3:19

TODAY'S WORD

My sister and I decided to visit Hot Springs, Arkansas. Our faith was tested as we boarded an eight-passenger plane. As we prayed for safe travels, God's word came to mind, "Do not be anxious about anything, but in every situation, by prayer and petition, with thanksgiving, present your requests to God" (Philippians 4:6). We relaxed and took in the bird's eye view of God's creation. The Lord was with us.

Throughout our trip, my sister and I had heartfelt conversations about our past and future as we hiked hills and walked city blocks. During the quiet times, God spoke to us individually about our hidden sins and burdens. We felt God's presence everywhere we went. One of the last places we visited was Gaven Woodland Gardens, the botanical garden of the University of Arkansas.

As we walked the trails with hundreds of others, my sister and I veered off the trail and walked a narrow path that led to a riverbank. For a moment, we were the only ones there. We were awestruck by the magnificent glory of God and began praising and thanking God for all He has done for us.

While wiping tears from our eyes and walking back to the trail, I remembered the scripture, "For my yoke is easy and my burden is light" (Matthew 11:30). We returned home from Hot Springs feeling lighter and refreshed. I thank the Holy Spirit for showing me that times of refreshing come from the presence of the Lord.

TODAY'S PRAYER

Lord God, I am in awe of all that You have created. Thank you for filling the earth with Your glory. I know that You are always with me and I need not fear.

Thank you for opening Your arms to draw me near to You. Your presence seeks to bring me peace and hope for my future.

When I confess my sins and turn to You, You give the gift of grace, love, and mercy. Help me to live in the freedom Your grace provides.

Help me, like Jesus, to seek solitude with You in quiet places to pray, praise and worship, release, and refresh. I am reminded of Isaiah 30:15, "…In repentance and rest is your salvation, in quietness and trust is your strength…"

Thank you for Your unconditional love. Keep me close to You always in the safety of Your love. Amen.

~Janice Lykes

Day #25

THROUGH THE FIRE

TODAY'S PASSAGE

My heart is stirred by a noble theme as I recite my verses for the king; my tongue is the pen of a skillful writer. Psalm 45:1

TODAY'S WORD

I am an extrovert. I receive energy from being around others. Simply put, I love to talk; few would describe me as quiet.

Two years ago, as I was walking to Dollar General, a car stopped and a man got out. He pointed a gun at me and demanded my bag. Quickly giving it to him, I ran home. A 15-second interaction rocked my world. Suddenly I couldn't talk. Literally. My world flipped instantaneously. Surely the pain would go away the next day, the next month. It didn't. Quickly I regained my speech, but it took months to get through the trauma.

Nothing surprises God. Not even armed robbery. The following months would have been catastrophic if I didn't believe God is who He says He is. Our heavenly Father is the ultimate comforter and healer. My faith and desperation for God grew. Firsthand, I learned about the fire He uses to refine us. It's one I never would have asked for, but am thankful I received.

Getting robbed at gunpoint seemed like the worst thing to ever happen to me; now I believe the opposite. Jesus never said He'd extinguish the flames, but He would hold our hand and walk through the fire with us. Through this traumatic event, Jesus revealed not only His character, but the one He put inside me.

TODAY'S PRAYER

God, thank you for being exactly who You say You are. You're the only one capable of bringing sunshine from darkness. Thank you for the constant love and companionship You offer for anyone who calls on Your name.

You take up as much space in our lives as we're willing to give You. You're in every detail. Nothing is too big for You, nor too small. You sent Your son, Jesus, so we may *have* life, and have it to the full (John 10:10).

I pray we're a people who surrender the pen to the author of our stories. I pray we let the Creator of Creation bring new life out of us, so we can do the same for others.

Show us what You mean by the words You wrote in Your book of life. It's in Your name I pray, amen.

~Kristen Ann Wiblishouser

Day #26

FORGIVING ME

TODAY'S PASSAGE

For the law of the Spirit of life has set you free in Christ Jesus from the law of sin and death.
Romans 8:2

TODAY'S WORD

Many years ago, my husband and I went through a nine-month inner healing course around forgiveness that greatly impacted us, both individually and as a couple. When someone hurts us, we learned to say, "I forgive you, even if you do it again, even if you never change."

When there was an injury, we spoke these words. Every single time, tears flowed from the one receiving forgiveness. Unconditional love is not familiar to us as human beings.

As believers, we often struggle the most with forgiving ourselves. Receiving the grace of God and extending it to others is not a problem. Why can't we let ourselves off the hook? Our expectations hold us hostage.

We carry around a heavy backpack of condemnation, self-hatred, and shame even while we go to church, share the gospel, and serve our families and communities. These unmet expectations, just like the law, produce death. Some examples are: "You should be skinnier, not on any medications, happier, sweeter, smarter, quieter, etc."

What if we applied unconditional love to ourselves? God accepts us just as we are. It's time to stop beating ourselves up.

Consider pleading the blood of Jesus over your body, mind, and heart daily. Look in the mirror and say, "I love you, even if you do it again, even if you never change."

May we allow the Holy Spirit to heal us in the deepest places where we feel we have fallen short. We are extravagantly loved and accepted by our heavenly Father!

TODAY'S PRAYER

Holy Spirit, reveal to us the areas in our hearts where we have held bitterness against ourselves.

We are often taught by our culture to hate our bodies and to focus on our shortcomings in work, in parenting, and in our relationships.

Please apply Your healing balm of grace to the wounds we have carried for far too long. We desire freedom from all laws that produce shame, condemnation, and rejection of self.

We receive Your acceptance, Your unconditional love, and we invite You to lift these burdens from us once and for all. In the mighty name of Jesus, amen.

~Rebekah McLeod

Day #27

JESUS WEEPS WITH US

TODAY'S PASSAGE

*Jesus said to her, "I am the resurrection and the life.
The one who believes in me will live, even though they die." John 11:25*

TODAY'S WORD

The flag-draped caisson rolls solemnly through fields planted with rows of tombstones. All is silent, save the patter of the horses' hoofbeats as they pull the wagon. I walk on, broken, in shock, following you – an Air National Guard Colonel – Daddy. The one who believed in Jesus. I stand at the precipice of a dark hole next to a mound of freshly dug frozen earth, dark against the white snow. Shots suddenly ring out in salute, the report reverberating off the hills, piercing my heart and echoing through the huge cavern in my soul. *Daddy! It's too cold to leave you here.* I shiver, remembering the warmth of his bear hug. *No mortal could ever hold, comfort, or care for me like you. You leave a great hole in my heart!*

Soldiers fold the flag into a triangle and press it into my trembling hands. *"…in the name of the Father, Son, and Holy Spirit."* The crimson stripes bleed through my eyes awash with tears. *Daddy! God brought you home from Vietnam, why not now? I didn't believe you were mortal!*

The lone bugler takes a deep breath, raising the bugle to his lips, the purest notes of "Taps" pour out. Another Daddy speaks to me, His words like powerful arms. *Your Daddy is safe with me.*

I am your Father now - I have always been your Father - I will always be your Father.

When you weep, God will also hold you in His arms of love.

TODAY'S PRAYER

Lord, thank you for weeping with us, just as You did for Lazarus. Death was not Your original plan, but because of sin, death entered the world. You remind us in Psalm 38:18 that You are "close to the brokenhearted and save those who are crushed in spirit."

Thank you for lifting our eyes and hearts at the grave when we grieve the loss of our loved ones who were like the sun in our sky. Please speak words of comfort, hope, and peace to every crushed heart.

For those who never made it home from a conflict, reassure their families they will be found, if not here on earth, then in heaven. Thank you for watching over the sparrow. How much more do You watch over the lives of Your children?

Psalm 56:8 says, "You keep track of all my sorrows. You have collected all my tears in Your bottle. You have recorded each one in your book."

None of our suffering is wasted. You wept over Lazarus' death, yet delayed in coming to his aid. Why? So all would see You truly are the Resurrection and the Life for all who believe (John 11:25). We do not mourn as those who have no hope (1 Thessalonians 4:13).

Because You were resurrected, the first fruits of Your new creation, we can entrust our loved ones to Your arms. Thank you for Your unspeakable joy in the hard places. Your Word brings life and hope as we keep our eyes on You.

~ Denise Arvaneh

Day #28

KINTSUGI THE HEART

TODAY'S PASSAGE

The Lord is close to the brokenhearted and saves those who are crushed in spirit.
Psalm 34:18

TODAY'S WORD

Kintsugi is the ancient art of fixing broken pottery with gold. In the 1400s, Japanese craftsmen started bonding together pieces of pottery by drawing attention to the break rather than away from it, making the break the most important part of the piece. This beautiful historic concept is now considered an important art form. It also teaches us to embrace beauty in our imperfections.

We are reminded that something can break and still be beautiful once repaired. It is stronger at the broken places. The broken object accepts its past and becomes more robust, more beautiful, and more precious than before. Like the golden fault lines running through Kintsugi, just as we are broken, we can be repaired.

God's healing is the golden bond that runs through the broken lines of our heart. Being so near to both sides, He can glue us back together calling attention to our brokenness rather than away from it. When God applies this Kintsugi method to our broken hearts, we become more beautiful, more robust, and more precious than ever, once repaired. Every broken piece is put back together with God's tender love, patience, and mercy. "I will sprinkle clean water on you… I will clean you from all your impurities…I will give you a new heart and put a new spirit in you. Then you will live!" (Ezekiel 36:25-28).

TODAY'S PRAYER

Heavenly Father, You are the Potter, and we are the clay. It does not matter how far into the process we have failed. You are able to make us more resilient, more precious, more purposeful than ever before.

I bring to You *all* my broken pieces, my broken relationships, my broken dreams, and even my broken faith.

Would you please Kintsugi my heart back together? Would you make it a masterpiece for Your glory?

Help me embrace my imperfections. Only You can put me back together again. Only You can finish the work You started in my life. You are the Alpha and the Omega, the beginning, and the end (Revelation 22:13).

I pray You will have Your way in my life today. In Jesus' name, amen.

~Elenor Quinones

Day #29

NO LONGER WEARY

TODAY'S PASSAGE

Come to me, all you who are weary and burdened, and I will give you rest. Matthew 11:28

TODAY'S WORD

Too many tasks and not enough time. It has become the American way, the way of the world. And it's wearing us out. Sleep disorders, insomnia, stress, tension, health-related issues, all because the weight of life has become too heavy.

As believers, the Bible reminds us we don't have to do it on our own. We have a Savior, Jesus, who carried the weight of the world on His shoulders. He is willing to carry our burdens today.

"Come to me, all you who are weary and burdened, and I will give you rest" (Matthew 11:28). This is Jesus' promise to us. If you are weary or burdened, He will exchange your load for sweet rest.

When I was in law school, the load I carried was heavy. As a full-time student, I was also working part-time for the university's Corporate Counsel, and balancing this with my husband's cancer battle. This might seem like more than one person could bear. You're right, I couldn't do it in my own strength. When I put it all in Jesus' hands, He showed me how to navigate through the battle zone.

Psalm 46:1 says, "God is our refuge and strength, an ever-present help in trouble." I ran to the Lord, often. Putting my husband, school, work, life – all of this and more in His hands. I was no longer weary. My burden was exchanged for His peace. His strength became my strength. Jesus will do the same for you.

TODAY'S PRAYER

Lord, we fall at Your feet with the messiness of our lives. The load is too heavy. Our arms are weak. Our hearts are weighed down. Our minds are unsettled as they hop from one concern to another.

In this moment, I turn my eyes away from the world, and fix my eyes on You, Lord Jesus. The love in Your eyes touches my heart before Your arms reach me. Just like a soft spring rain, my soul once dry and withered comes to life.

My breathing is no longer shallow and rapid. The pneuma breath of life fills my lungs. My heart beats with Your heart according to the unforced rhythm of Your grace.

"For my thoughts are not your thoughts, neither are your ways my ways," declares the LORD. As the heavens are higher than the earth, so are my ways higher than your ways and my thoughts than your thoughts" (Isaiah 55:8-9).

Here we find hope because we know Your best will prevail. You place a blanket of peace on my shoulders. It is not heavy, it is light. Your peace that passes all understanding guards my heart and mind.

Thank you, Jesus, for carrying me. Victory is mine! I am no longer weary. In Jesus' name, amen.

~ Barbara Hollace

Day #30

SADNESS WITH HOPE

TODAY'S PASSAGE

"For I know the plans I have for you," declares the LORD, *"plans to prosper you and not to harm you, plans to give you hope and a future." Jeremiah 29:11*

TODAY'S WORD

When I was 30 years old, I went to work on a cruise ship, where I met a charming, polite, South African man. After working 15 days together, we fell in love. Six months later, we were married. I was an Argentinian woman living her dream. My prayers were answered.

After nine years of marriage and God's gift of our son, my husband passed away suddenly. He was only 41 years old. While my husband was in a coma, I prayed for God's will. Even though I had faith, something died inside when he passed. I found myself holding onto God but had no hope. I didn't know what to pray.

"Lord, I got everything I was praying for, everything I waited for, and now? You got it all. I have nothing else that I hoped for. My life with my husband and son was my big picture."

When I had no strength, I remember praying, "May the same power that raised Christ Jesus from the dead, raise me up" and "I can do all things through Him who strengthens me." Day after day, I found myself waking up earlier, gaining strength and motivation to get up and leave my bed, not just for the daily obligations, but to *live*!

The "new big picture" may not be figured out, my struggles aren't over, but my sadness is now mixed with hope. Every day I pray that God will raise me up to His purpose, His new hope, not mine.

TODAY'S PRAYER

Lord, when we walk through places of sorrow, You are with us. You tell us that we can do *all* things through Christ who strengthens us (Philippians 4:13).

Holy Spirit, remind us of God's promise that we are raised to new life in Christ. Do a makeover in our lives. Turn our mourning into dancing and our sorrow into joy.

"For since we believe that Jesus died and was raised to life again, we also believe that when Jesus returns, God will bring back with him the believers who have died. And now, dear brothers and sisters, we want you to know what will happen to the believers who have died so you will not grieve like people who have no hope. We tell you this directly from the Lord: We who are still living when the Lord returns will not meet him ahead of those who have died. For the Lord himself will come down from heaven with a commanding shout, with the voice of the archangel, and with the trumpet call of God. First, the believers who have died will rise from their graves. Then, together with them, we who are still alive and remain on the earth will be caught up in the clouds to meet the Lord in the air. Then we will be with the Lord forever. So, encourage each other with these words" (1 Thessalonians 4:13-18).

Let the hope which was lost, be renewed in Him. In Jesus' name, amen.

~ Graciela Trovato

> Therefore, since we are surrounded by such a great cloud of witnesses, let us throw off everything that hinders and the sin that so easily entangles. And let us run with perseverance the race marked out for us, fixing our eyes on Jesus, the pioneer and perfecter of faith. For the joy set before him he endured the cross, scorning its shame, and sat down at the right hand of the throne of God. Consider him who endured such opposition from sinners, so that you will not grow weary and lose heart.
>
> ~ Hebrews 12:1-3

He Died so You could Live.

Receive His Gift of Eternal Life.

Embrace His Love. Experience His Joy.

Find Hope. Be Filled with Peace.

Walk with Jesus on His final 10-day Journey to the Cross.

Day #31
DOES GOD TRUST YOU?

TODAY'S PASSAGE

You prepare a table before me in the presence of my enemies. You anoint my head with oil; my cup overflows. Psalm 23:5

TODAY'S WORD

The words of Psalm 23 are familiar to almost everyone – no matter your religious preference. Often they are spoken at the end of someone's life, but also a great comfort through a person's lifetime. When David wrote Psalm 23, he was an experienced shepherd. The words paint the story of his life and the comfort David found from God. And also, the comfort David brought his own sheep.

In April 2020, as my husband came to the end of his life's journey, the Good Shepherd was there, not only to usher my husband into the glory of heaven, but to comfort me.

When our pastor arrived, he spoke these words, "God must really trust you." In that moment, I wasn't really sure what they meant. But I came to realize walking through hard places is reserved for those God knows can be trusted.

"Even though I walk through the darkest valley, I will fear no evil, for you are with me; your rod and your staff, they comfort me" (Psalm 23:4).

It is not a punishment, but rather a privilege to be entrusted with such a sacred honor. There is no fear in God's presence. There is only His comfort and joy, unspeakable and indescribable.

You may be walking through a dark valley. Do not fear. Take the Good Shepherd's hand and let Him lead you back to the green pastures where you will find rest for your soul (Psalm 23:2-3). You can trust Him.

TODAY'S PRAYER

Heavenly Father, we thank you for the gift of Your love. We are grateful that life isn't just one-dimensional. There are hills and valleys, rain and sunshine, joy and sorrow, grace and gratefulness. All of it points us back to You, the giver of every good and perfect gift.

We know that You are trustworthy because You have a 100% success rate of getting us to the place in our lives we are right now. Your love never fails (1 Corinthians 13:8).

Be with those going through the darkest valley today – in their home, relationships, workplace, church, school, hospital, wherever life is hard. We are grateful You are the Miracle Worker. You make a way where there doesn't seem to be a way. Open their eyes, Lord, to see You are with them, that they are not alone.

We are reminded in scripture that we can trust You, Lord. Proverbs 3:5-6 says, "Trust in the LORD with all your heart and lean not on your own understanding; in all your ways submit to him, and he will make your paths straight."

Thank you for trusting us to walk through our challenges as good ambassadors of Your love and faithfulness. May we praise God in the storms of life until the morning dawns and we find we have made it safely into Your arms of love. We love you, Lord. In Jesus' name we pray, amen.

~ Barbara Hollace

Day #32

WHAT CAN I OFFER?

TODAY'S PASSAGE

All these people gave their gifts out of their wealth; but she out of her poverty put in all she had to live on. Luke 21:4

TODAY'S WORD

In my current circumstances, I don't think there is much I can offer God. I'm not wealthy and I have few possessions. I have no position or reputation. In my mind, nothing of consequence. All I can offer God is my "yes." A yes to follow Him in every circumstance.

Choosing to follow and love Jesus is not necessarily an easy choice. When I am lost and broken, it is really hard to surrender. In times of suffering, my heart, actions, and words do not align. In these dark moments, I am faced with the decision to trust and love Him at all times.

I'm still praying for my breakthrough in certain areas. The battles are fierce and constant. The thought of quitting creeps in. Then I have to make the decision to stop or press on. This is when I offer God the shattered bits of me and ask the Lord to help me to endure. When I feel like I am in a deficit, but give myself wholly to Him, it is the sweetest and most genuine kind of offering.

Like the widow who gave two very small copper coins, I want Jesus to know that I did not give out of my wealth, but in my poverty I put in all that I had to live on. At the end of my life, I want to hear my Lord say, "Well done, good and faithful servant!" (Matthew 25:23).

TODAY'S PRAYER

Lord, I want to love You with all my heart, soul, strength, and mind (Matthew 22:37). I give all of me to You. This offering is an expression of my love for You. You are worthy of my love.

There is truly no one like You. I declare, "Holy, holy, holy is the Lord God Almighty, who was, and is and is to come" (Revelation 4:8).

As Job prayed, I pray, "Naked I came from my mother's womb and naked I will depart. The Lord gave and the Lord has taken away; may the name of the Lord be praised" (Job 1:21).

Everything I have belongs to You. Use it for Your kingdom to bless many.

~ Shalley Kim

Day #33

CHOOSING THE RIGHT PATH

TODAY'S PASSAGE

Do not conform to the pattern of this world, but be transformed by the renewing of your mind. Then you will be able to test and approve what God's will is—his good, pleasing and perfect will. Romans 12:2

TODAY'S WORD

What we think about often determines the path we take. How many times has temptation led us to a place we shouldn't be? Whether that was in front of the refrigerator or binge-watching television, or other activities that were not life-giving.

"Do not conform to the pattern of this world, but be transformed by the renewing of your mind. Then you will be able to test and approve what God's will is—his good, pleasing and perfect will" (Romans 12:2). God created us to stand out from the world and be transformed. 1 Corinthians 2:16 tells us "we have the mind of Christ." God gives us the opportunity to choose the path that makes us more like Jesus.

As I walked out my own health journey, there were lots of decisions to make. Not only medical decisions, but where I focused my attention. Would I stand on the promises of God or be swayed by the opinions of man? Many times, I went to the Lord in prayer and asked Him to direct my path to His "good, pleasing and perfect will." It was not always the popular, easy path but it always brought God honor and glory.

Jesus did the same in the Garden of Gethsemane. The cross was before Him, all its pain and agony. "Father, if you are willing, take this cup from me; yet not my will, but yours be done" (Luke 22:42). May we have the courage to follow Jesus' steps of obedience.

TODAY'S PRAYER

Lord, thank you for the gift of Your amazing grace. We can't take the next step on our journey without it. As followers of Jesus, You call us away from the crowd to a straight and narrow path. Jesus, by Your example, You have shown us what it looks like to listen and obey.

God always has the best in mind for us. "This is what the LORD says – your Redeemer, the Holy One of Israel: 'I am the LORD your God, who teaches you what is best for you, who directs you in the way you should go'" (Isaiah 48:17).

Thank you for the Holy Spirit who guides and comforts us on our life's journey. Lord, we want to know Your will and what is best for us. Open our eyes to see and our ears to hear Your still, small voice as it calls us to be more like You.

Be with those who are in their own Garden of Gethsemane moment as they wrestle with God's will versus their will in hard places. We are more than conquerors through Him who loved us (Romans 8:37). May Your Kingdom come. Your will be done on earth, as it is in heaven. In Jesus' name, amen.

~ Barbara Hollace

Day #34

RUNNING THE RACE

TODAY'S PASSAGE

Therefore, since we are surrounded by such a great cloud of witnesses, let us throw off everything that hinders and the sin that so easily entangles. And let us run with perseverance the race marked out for us. Hebrews 12:1

TODAY'S WORD

Whether you are an athlete or not, young or old, you are running the race called life. Children love to run, especially if they're playing a game. You can hear their laughter echoing through the neighborhood. Life is not lived alone; it is lived out on a stage. We all have a platform. It's a place God has chosen for us from the beginning of time.

In Hebrews 12:1, we see a beautiful picture of this race. "Therefore, since we are surrounded by such a great cloud of witnesses, let us throw off everything that hinders and the sin that so easily entangles. And let us run with perseverance the race marked out for us."

It reminds me of a childhood memory. After practicing running at school, it was time to show my family how fast I could run. Arriving at the playground, I was ready to run like the wind. Until I fell, and skinned my knees on the blacktop. Proverbs 24:16 reminds us we will fall but we get back up and continue the race.

On the way to the cross, Jesus fell too, under the weight of the load. God sent someone to help Jesus carry the cross (Mark 15:21). The Holy Spirit will guide and comfort you on your race. You do not have to bear the weight alone; Jesus already paid the price. A great cloud of witnesses is cheering you on, here on earth and in heaven.

TODAY'S PRAYER

Lord, thank you that You promised to never leave us or forsake us (Deuteronomy 31:6). Wherever You lead us, You have equipped us.

We are not running this race alone. Jesus, You have gone before us to smooth the way. A great cloud of witnesses is watching our every step.

You remind us in Hebrews 12:2 that we should be "fixing our eyes on Jesus, the pioneer and perfecter of faith. For the joy set before him he endured the cross, scorning its shame, and sat down at the right hand of the throne of God."

Jesus is sitting in a place of victory. With joy, He endured the cross, and overcame its shame because of His great love for us. May we find the same joy in the trials we face. We must strip away the things that hinder us because Jesus has taught us how to run the race, and run it well.

Keep our feet from stumbling, Lord. We are grateful that You neither slumber nor sleep (Psalm 121:3). God's eyes of love are upon you. Lord, we want to finish our race well. In Jesus' name we pray, amen.

~ Barbara Hollace

Day #35

KNOWN BY SCARS

TODAY'S PASSAGE

Then he said to Thomas, "Put your finger here; see my hands. Reach out your hand and put it into my side. Stop doubting and believe." John 20:27

TODAY'S WORD

I think it's natural to have questions and doubts. Most of us can't take someone's word, we need to personally experience it. Although Jesus said to Thomas, "Blessed are those who have not seen, and have believed" (John 20:29), Jesus still appeared to Thomas in a way that he needed to be met. How wonderful that Jesus wants a personal relationship with us.

After hearing reports of Jesus' resurrection, Thomas declared, "Unless I see the nail marks in his hands and put my finger where the nails were, and put my hand into his side, I will not believe" (John 20:25). In His kindness, Jesus let Thomas touch His scars. The way Thomas felt may be similar to how I feel touching my dad's hands.

The wrinkles and calluses show that my father used his hands to provide for his family. He has a visible scar from surgery because his fingers became deformed from so much use. Hands that took so much so I could have a better future. Holding my father's hands with their bumps and hardened layers comforts me.

When Thomas felt Jesus' hands and side, it wasn't just proof that He was in front of him. The scars were reminders of how much Jesus loved Thomas and how Jesus overcame the biggest devastation and disappointment in his life. That is the beauty of Jesus' resurrection, wounds are no longer signs of pain and doubt but of hope and comfort.

TODAY'S PRAYER

Lord, I confess that in the waiting, I allow my fears and doubts to overwhelm me. Forgive me when I lose sight of You. When I begin to distrust You, hold me close. In difficult times, guard my heart so it does not stray from You.

Thank you for being a God who knows me, even the number of hairs on my head (Luke 12:7). In return, may I learn more about You, Your ways, and Your timing. I want to know You more.

May the scars in my life be a marker and testament to Your faithfulness. My confidence is in You and not the things of the world. As I wait for You, help me to wait with hope. Even though I may struggle, may my faith endure and not give up.

As You told Thomas, "Blessed are those who have not seen, and have believed" (John 20:29).

And as Peter told the church in Asia Minor, "Though you have not seen him, you love him; and even though you do not see him now, you believe in him and are filled with an inexpressible and glorious joy, for you are receiving the end result of your faith, the salvation of your souls" (1 Peter 1:8-9).

May we be ones who love You even when we can't see You. Fill us with the Holy Spirit as we hold onto the joy of our salvation. Amen.

~ Shalley Kim

Day #36

SPIRIT OF ADOPTION

TODAY'S PASSAGE

I will not leave you as orphans; I will come to you. John 14:18

TODAY'S WORD

It may sound silly but I learned a lot about love and grace from my dog. As a puppy, Copper was afraid to be left alone. If I stepped away, he would bark and go crazy. I had to teach him that he would be okay when I was not around.

Putting Copper's favorite toys next to him, I walked away. When I returned, he got a treat. Eventually, I increased the steps until I could walk out the door. As Copper began to trust that I would come back, he didn't act like a fearful dog, he became brave.

As I look back on my life, I often felt alone. I was living with an orphan mentality. That's what the enemy does – he comes after your identity. When you live with an orphan spirit, you operate out of fear and shame. You think you will never have enough. You think you will never be good enough. And if you don't know your worth, you'll feel like you are always alone.

Thank goodness we have a God who wants to be a father to the fatherless (Psalm 68:5). And in His kindness, He gave us the Holy Spirit who comes to our defense and gives us protection.

He is our best advocate. I no longer have to perform to receive love or affirm my value. God loves me simply for being me. We are not alone because we are His.

TODAY'S PRAYER

You love me as a loving Father. You love me intimately. I am loved and accepted. I do not have to earn Your love. Thank you for demonstrating Your love for me.

Even though I am a sinner, You died for me (Romans 5:8). I trust You to lead me. You will not abandon me. You are with me in good times and bad times.

Break the orphan spirit in me and help me live with the spirit of adoption. I do not have to do things alone. I do not have to build my own success.

Holy Spirit, thank you for working in my life. Guide my steps, my thoughts, and my heart. Help me see myself the way You see me. You say I am loveable.

May these feelings of being discarded, undesired, or rejected be replaced with love and acceptance. I declare that Your goodness and love will follow me all the days of my life (Psalm 23:6).

~ Shalley Kim

Day #37

SUBMIT, SURRENDER, SACRIFICE

TODAY'S PASSAGE

But if serving the LORD seems undesirable to you, then choose for yourselves this day whom you will serve… But as for me and my household, we will serve the LORD. Joshua 24:15

TODAY'S WORD

No more sitting on the fence. Either you're in or you're out. You get to decide. There are crossroads in our lives where we must decide to choose our way or God's way, our will or God's will. It looks simple on paper but often we wrestle with this decision.

At Shechem, Joshua poses a question to the people asking them to choose whom they would serve. Before they respond, he boldly states his position, "But as for me and my household, we will serve the Lord" (Joshua 24:15b). There was no doubt where Joshua stood.

In 2018, there was a crossroad in my life, when my second husband entered the hospital with some major health challenges. Conditions that threatened to take his life. God asked me that first day, January 10, 2018, to step up and boldly declare where I stood. My heavenly Father asked me to be transparent about our journey – our struggles and God's faithfulness for all to see. Social media was a place God wanted to influence and we were His chosen people.

In that moment, God asked me to submit everything I had to Him – my past, present, and future. And to surrender my will for His will, no matter the outcome. My heavenly Father made it clear there would be sacrifices on this journey. The path would not be without pain but there was a purpose. I chose to serve the Lord and to honor Him, without reservation, and still do today.

TODAY'S PRAYER

Lord, we come with humble hearts filled with thanksgiving because of the great sacrifice Jesus made on our behalf. Jesus went to the cross for me. He laid down everything. Jesus left the glory of heaven and became a man so He could pay the price for my sins, all our sins.

His sacrifice was great, greater than anything I will be asked to sacrifice. It cost Jesus His life, crucifixion on a cross, bearing the weight and shame for all of mankind. All of this because of His great love for us.

Today, God, You are asking us to choose where we stand. Are we for You or against You? Will we choose the temporary pleasures of this world or the eternal riches of glory?

Lord, we surrender all to You today. We choose to walk with You on this life journey. "You will show me the path of life; in Your presence is fullness of joy; at Your right hand are pleasures forevermore" (Psalm 16:11 NJKV).

Be with those we love who are sitting on the fence or wandering in the darkness.

Good Shepherd, bring them back where there is safety in Your arms of love. We will give You all the praise and honor and glory in Jesus' mighty name, amen.

~ Barbara Hollace

Day #38

PROMISE OF HEAVEN

TODAY'S PASSAGE

And if I go and prepare a place for you, I will come back and take you to be with me that you also may be where I am. John 14:3

TODAY'S WORD

From the ground, the human eye sees only a fraction of a rainbow. Did you know that a rainbow is not an arc? From a higher vantage point, the rainbow is actually a full circle.

In Genesis 9, God tells Noah the rainbow is a sign of His covenant that He would not destroy all creation by flood again. We can enjoy God and all He has here on earth. But He does not stop there. In John 14, Jesus talks about a new covenant, a covenant that promises us eternal life.

Do we fully grasp God's promise? I have to admit, I live a life of drudgery. The injustices of the world often get me down. My focus is very earthly bound.

If I truly understood the promises of heaven, I wouldn't carry so much fear and brokenness. Instead of an earthly view, I need a new perspective – a heavenly one. With a heavenly perspective, you can't have a defeatist attitude.

Let us rise on eagles' wings and take the higher view. "For those who hope in the Lord will renew their strength. They will soar on wings like eagles; they will run and not grow weary, they will walk and not be faint" (Isaiah 40:31).

Heaven is our home. Since we know we have eternal life, let us live fearlessly here on earth from a place of strength.

TODAY'S PRAYER

Lord, You said, "Heaven is my throne, and the earth is my footstool. Where is the house you will build for me? Where will my resting place be?" (Isaiah 66:1).

Lord, let Your resting place be in me. I invite You into my life. Rest in me. Live in me. I lift up my eyes to the mountains – where does my help come from? My help comes from the Lord, the Maker of heaven and earth (Psalm 121:1-2).

I fix my eyes on You because I am confident You will come to help and save me. You have called us to rise on eagles' wings. Help me to focus on You and take the higher view.

Give us power over our circumstances. Help us to live fearlessly. Give us heavenly vision. Help us not to see things from our own vantage point but help us to see with Your eyes and Your heart.

We live not to build a kingdom here but Your kingdom in heaven.

~ Shalley Kim

Day #39

IT IS FINISHED

TODAY'S PASSAGE

When he had received the drink, Jesus said, "It is finished." With that, he bowed his head and gave up his spirit. John 19:30

TODAY'S WORD

I'm not very different from the Israelites. I've grumbled and complained because things were too hard. The Israelites left Egypt thinking they would enter the Promised Land quickly and without a fight. But the journey was long! They were tired and impatient, and began speaking against the Lord.

In response, He sent venomous snakes that bit the people and many Israelites died. Then the people cried out again, repenting of their sins and begged Moses to pray for them. As Moses prayed, the Lord told him to make a snake out of copper and put it on a pole. When people looked at it, they were healed.

While the Israelites had a copper snake on a pole, believers today can look upon the cross that held Jesus. Our healing begins when we look up to the cross. On the cross, Jesus took all our sins and punishment on Himself. We no longer have to look to a copper snake on a pole, or sacrifices, or temples, because Jesus redeemed and reconciled us. This act of love cost Jesus His life. Remember Jesus cried out, *"Eloi, Eloi, lema sabachthani?"* which means "My God, my God, why have you forsaken me?" (Matthew 27:46). Though the sacrifice was great, Jesus finished what He came to do.

When you think the Lord might have abandoned you because your journey has been too hard and too long, look to the cross.

TODAY'S PRAYER

Lord, when I am tired and impatient, help me look to You. Open my eyes. Help me to see who You really are. Forgive me for the times I have taken You for granted. I am sorry I grumbled when You gave me manna. I looked at my lack instead of what You provided.

I confess sometimes I think my ways are better. You say, "For my thoughts are not your thoughts, neither are your ways my ways," declares the Lord. "As the heavens are higher than the earth, so are my ways higher than your ways and my thoughts than your thoughts" (Isaiah 55:8-9).

You are for us. Trouble, hardship, persecution, famine, danger, or sword can't keep us away from You. Through You, we are more than conquerors. Nothing can separate us from You (Romans 8:31-39).

Thank you for the cross. You did not deserve to die a humiliating death. There was so much pain, so much agony, but it didn't stop You. Instead, You endured it all for me. You are the resurrection and the life. Anyone who believes in You will live and whoever lives by believing in You will never die (John 11:25-26).

I believe in You. I put my trust in You. You finished it all on the cross. I don't have to go looking for other things to make me complete. I look to You. In my sweet Jesus' name I pray, amen.

~ Shalley Kim

Day #40

GREATER THINGS TO COME

TODAY'S PASSAGE

Very truly I tell you, whoever believes in me will do the works I have been doing, and they will do even greater things than these, because I am going to the Father. John 14:12

TODAY'S WORD

Saying good-bye is difficult, whether it's for a moment or a lifetime. Where there is great love, there is a powerful heart connection.

Jesus, the Son of God, came into the world as a little baby. In the final scene, His life comes to a powerful conclusion. The cross loomed before Jesus, not the ending His disciples expected. Jesus saw beyond the cross and attempted to prepare them.

"Very truly I tell you, whoever believes in me will do the works I have been doing, and they will do even greater things than these, because I am going to the Father" (John 14:12).

In truth, Jesus saw you and me, generations later. We were part of the joy Jesus focused on those last days of His life. This promise to His disciples is His promise to us too.

When I have walked through seasons of loss, it's difficult to see beyond my broken heart. For a moment, I am stuck. Hearing the words of my future assignment takes my breath away.

"There is no fear in love. But perfect love drives out fear" (1 John 4:18a). Just like Jesus' disciples, the resurrection power of Jesus lives in me as I follow Him. I am equipped for this journey.

Will you choose to believe Jesus has greater things in store for you? The cross is not the end of His story. Jesus is the resurrected Christ who overcame death, hell, and the grave. He's alive forevermore!

TODAY'S PRAYER

Heavenly Father, thank you for the gift of Jesus. You sent Your only son to bear the weight of our sins and endure much suffering. As we have walked with Jesus, in the days preceding the cross, we have been witnesses to the magnitude of this gift.

His suffering was not without hope. Jesus saw beyond the cross. You call us to do the same. We know the rest of the story about His resurrection and triumph over death. Help us to choose daily to walk in His steps of victory.

Fill our hearts with joy even through difficult seasons. May we be wrapped in a blanket of Your peace where the cares of life cannot penetrate the shield of Your love.

"The Lord is our shepherd, we lack nothing" (Psalm 23:1). That is the truth and we will stand on it. We welcome the greater things You have for us because we understand You will take our hand and walk with us.

"Jesus looked at them and said, 'With man this is impossible, but with God all things are possible'" (Matthew 19:26).

Risen Savior, we receive this gift from Your hands and Your heart. We receive the miracles You have in mind for us. In the name of Jesus, we ask all these things, amen.

~ Barbara Hollace

The Rest of the Story… the Hope of Jesus

As you come to the end of this 40-day devotional, you are face to face with the cross where Jesus died. You have walked the path of suffering with Him. You have also read our stories of places where God met us, just ordinary people, in our times of trouble.

The Christ of Calvary becomes the victorious risen Christ just three days after His crucifixion. Jesus was not left on the cross.

The mission He came to accomplish was completed. The transaction to pay for our sins and shortcomings was marked paid in full by our heavenly Father. Heaven is our reward thanks to Jesus.

Hope in the Waiting is more than the title of this book, it's the truth we can hold on to as we encounter tests, trials, and temptations. You may be waiting for your miracle. The wait has been long. Just like Thomas, you may be doubting that you will ever be healed, or your family restored, or your finances will meet your needs.

There is hope in the name of the Lord. Hold on to hope. Hold on to Jesus' hand and He will guide you to victory!

The Power of Prayer

Prayer is our invitation to God to intervene in the affairs of earth. It is our request for Him to work His ways in this world. ~ Myles Monroe

Prayer warriors pray, it's what they do best. Praying without ceasing is not just a Bible verse (1 Thessalonians 5:17), it's a way of life.

The women in our prayer pod are devout prayer warriors. Our prayers do not hit the ceiling and fall to the floor. They hit their mark. God recognizes our voices as we storm heaven's gates with prayers for ourselves and others.

In 2023, we saw answered prayers in so many areas. Here is just a small sampling of where God was on the move.

A woman, adopted as a child, had been looking for over 20 years for her birth family. God answered her prayers! She was introduced to a God-fearing family who welcomed her with tears of joy and praises to God's name.

Several medical events including a spider bite healed without any further infection along with the reduction of the hospital bill and minimal days off work. A young woman's neurosurgery was finally okayed by the insurance company and was successful. The family needed a six-figure miracle. God provided an independent arbitrator who ruled in their favor. Also hernia surgery for an 87-year-old man, no infection or swelling, just renewed strength. Thank you, Lord. He is Jehovah Rapha, our healer, and Jehovah Jireh, our provider.

God cares about work colleagues and tense relationships too. After two years of prayer, a work colleague asked if they could start over again, begin a new chapter, and start collaborating.

From helping with making a large family move while balancing other commitments to finding employment after a retiree's 10-year search, God has shown Himself to be faithful. Nothing is too big or too small for Him. Your concerns are God's concerns.

We also saw two prayers find their solution within our group. One woman looking for a person to join her real estate team and another young woman looking for a job and a fresh start. God brought them together for such a time as this. Two prayers answered as God continues to write the rest of the story to give them hope and a future.

Do you know the power of prayer in your own life? Our prayer is that you have been inspired to seek God's face with your own circumstances, big or small. God's ears are tuned to hear the cries of your heart. Seek His face today.

List of Authors

Rosalind Able lives in Memphis, Tennessee.
Penne Allison lives in Memphis, Tennessee.
Denise Arvaneh lives in Severn, Maryland.
Terrah A. Dews lives in Maryland.
JoEllen Delamatta lives in Centreville, Virginia.
Liv Dooley lives in Las Vegas, Nevada.
Liz Etim lives in Michigan.
Anastassia Geiger lives in Fairbanks, Alaska.
Linda Cawthon Griffin lives in Pittsburgh, Pennsylvania.
Pastor Valarie Grimes lives in Savannah, Georgia.
Jenna Marie Higgins lives in Magnolia, Massachusetts.
Barbara Hollace lives in Spokane Valley, Washington.
Adrienne Howell lives in Ohio.
Carolann Jones lives in New Jersey.
Shalley Kim lives in Gaithersburg, Maryland.
Janice Lykes lives in Lansing, Michigan.
Greta McHaney-Trice lives in Lansing, Michigan.
Rebekah McLeod lives in Savannah, Georgia.
Sharon McWilliams lives in Lansing, Michigan.
Morenike Ogebe lives in Springfield, Virginia.
Elenor Quinones lives in Florida.
Octavia Shaw-Williams lives in Washington DC.
Emra Smith lives in Rincon, Georgia.
Kieu Smith lives in Washington DC.
JoJo Stansfield lives in Shady Side, Maryland.
Nicole Thompson lives in Washington DC.
Graciela Trovato lives in Puerto Madryn, Argentina.
G Washington lives in Greenbelt, Maryland.
Kristen Ann Wiblishouser lives in Harwood, Maryland.

Thank you!

Be joyful in hope, patient in affliction, faithful in prayer. Romans 12:12

We are grateful to God for His steadfast love and faithfulness. This book would not be in your hands without a vision from God through the Holy Spirit.

As we walk through the Lent season, Christ's suffering is only part of the story. The resurrection of Jesus Christ gives us hope as we walk this road to the cross.

Special thanks to Anastassia Geiger who used her beautiful artistic talent to paint our book cover. God will bless you as you continue to wait on Him for your long-awaited miracles.

Ann Mathews is a priceless member of our team as she uses her formatting and design skills for God's honor and glory.

To each woman who took a leap of faith and shared a story of God's presence in her life, we applaud your boldness and courage. Our God will reward you.

Jesus, without Your love and sacrifice, we would have no hope. Instead, our eternity is secure.

To God be the glory great things He has done, and greater things are yet to come!

Barb & Shalley

www.ingramcontent.com/pod-product-compliance
Lightning Source LLC
LaVergne TN
LVHW020936090426
835512LV00020B/3386